Yesterdays
and
Tomorrows

Yesterdays and Tomorrows

PATIENCE STRONG

MULLER
London   Sydney   Auckland   Johannesburg

This edition first published in 1992 by Muller

Random Century Group Ltd
20 Vauxhall Bridge Road, London SW1V 2SA

Random Century Australia (Pty) Ltd
20 Alfred Street, Milsons Point, Sydney, NSW 2061, Australia

Random Century New Zealand Ltd
PO Box 40–086, Glenfield, Auckland 10, New Zealand

Random Century South Africa (Pty) Ltd
PO Box 337, Bergvlei, 2012, South Africa

British Library Cataloguing in Publication Data
Strong, Patience
  Yesterdays and tomorrows.
  I. Title
  242

  ISBN 0–09–175174–8

Set in Bembo by 🗡 Tek Art Ltd,
Addiscombe, Croydon, Surrey
Printed and bound in Great Britain by
Biddles Ltd, Guildford and King's Lynn

Contents

a=1st poem on page
b=2nd poem on page

Visiting Hours

How much they mean, how sweet they are to those who have
to lie
Week in, week out in hospital and how the minutes fly!
When neighbours, friends or relatives appear beside the bed.
All too quickly comes the time when goodbyes must be said.

They come, they go, and you are left your own thoughts to
pursue
Thinking over all the bits of news they bring to you.
From a life that seems to be a thousand miles away
From the little world in which you live from day to day
Hoping, praying, wondering how long it's going to be
Before you're ready to go home, before you're fit and free.

Underneath the Earth

Under the earth the bulbs lie deep,
Buried in their winter sleep.
Under the frosts the seeds are sealed
In garden bed and furrowed field.
Under a shroud of seeming death
They wait for April's warming breath:
Iris, tulips, crocuses,
Daffodils, anemones.

In the hard unyielding ground,
The sapless roots are locked and bound.
Below the crust of morning time,
Nature dormant bides her time.
Lilac, lily, cherry, may
Await their resurrection day.

Yesterdays and Tomorrows

God of my yesterdays, I have forgotten
All that I failed in when put to the test.
Yet somewhere the whole of my life is recorded
Things unremembered and still unconfessed.
Time buries much and the years fly so fast,
I'll need Thy forgiveness if judged on the past.

God of the future and times not yet planned
All my tomorrows still rest in Thy hand;
The moments, the hours and the days yet to be
Are veiled from my view but are known unto Thee . . .
Thou seest the place where the road will be hard.
Go Thou before me, my Guide and my Guard.

The Vigil

When you watch beside the bed of someone who is ill,
In the dark and silent time when all the house is still,
You keep your vigil hour by hour. The world outside seems
dead.
You pray for strength and cling to hope, although it's just a
thread.

But when the first faint gleam of dawn dispels the night's cold
gloom,
New life comes in with the early light that steals about the
room.
How welcome is the morning as the shadows fade away.
How sweet it is to know God has sent another day.

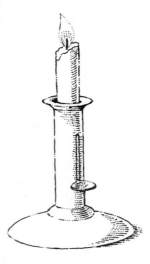

Taking Things Well

You have to learn to take things and to take them humorously.
A blow, a knock, a jibe, a shock, whatever it may be.
You have to take what hits you in the course of every day,
Learning how to take things in a gay, good-natured way.

You have to learn to take some pricks and maybe lots of stings.
You cannot go through life escaping the unpleasant things . . .
Someone's bound to hurt your feelings, but although it's hard,
Never let them see the tears or catch you off your guard.

A Birthday Wish

Down sunlit pathways may you travel all through life, my
                                                      friend,
With hope to light your morning way and peace at journey's
                                                        end.
Though storms may gather here and there and mists obscure
                                                   the view,
May you never fail to find a little patch of blue.

This my wish for you, that you will have the power to see
A bright horizon through the storm-clouds of adversity.
For if you bring a happy heart to each experience,
You will always walk the sunlit paths of Providence.

June Bride

Married in the month of roses when the year is in its prime,
And all Nature is rejoicing in the glow of summertime.
Married in the lovely season when the sun is high and bright,
When the air is sweet and fragrant and the days are long and
light.

Happy be the bride of June, not only on her wedding day,
But may she have the joy we wish her all the while and all the
way.
May she cherish in her heart this glad and glorious memory –
To keep the flame of love alight through the years that are to
be.

The Sunshine House

Make your house a sunshine house and open windows wide.
When the air is fresh and fragrant let it get inside.
Do not shut it out, but let it blow into your room,
Bringing in the sound of songbirds and the scent of bloom.

Even though you live where there's a grey and gloomy view,
You yourself can be a window that the sun gleams through . . .
Make your life a House of Sunshine, cheery, bright and gay:
A life that shines and gives out light to all who pass your way.

The Day We Met

If I could live one day again, one day out of the past,
I'd choose the day that we two met, for when my mind I cast
Across the landscape of the years, it stands out bright and bold.
The memory is evergreen, although the tale is old.

A lovely summer afternoon, a blue and golden sky.
A garden by the water and a white sail moving by . . .
And someone coming up the path I'd never seen before –
Walking straight into my life to stay for evermore.

First Love

First love is a precious thing that comes when all the world is
new.
The bloom of Springtime is upon it and the sheen of morning
dew.

First love often ends in heartaches . . . cruel then this life can
seem,
Looked at through the broken windows of a lost and lovely
dream.

When we're young the first sweet passion is a pleasure tinged
with pain . . .
And when it dies, we never think that we shall ever love
again.

Something Happens

We think we've got our lives all figured out.
We face the future sanguine and serene.
We think we know just what it's all about –
Then something happens, something unforeseen.

It doesn't do to plan too carefully.
To be too sure, too clever, or too wise.
For often things work out quite differently.
God takes a hand and springs a big surprise.

Sentiment

Why do we love to keep old letters, hiding them away
In a corner where we keep our dreams of yesterday?
Can it be because we find it hard to make a break
With some recollection kept alive for old times' sake?

Memories are made of unseen threads and silken strands,
Yet they bind us closely like the grip of iron bands.
Fondly do we treasure as the changing years advance
Letters that recall the days of youth and of romance.

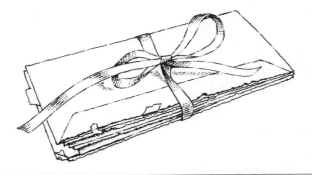

Wonderful Day

If you're looking for things to be awkward about then you
won't have to look very far.
A hundred excuses for making complaints you can find on the
spot where you are.
Life hands you a grievance as soon as you rise, if your thoughts
take that natural line.
There'll always be something to start you off grumbling if you
are determined to whine.

Don't let it happen. As soon as you wake, get your mind in the
right sort of frame.
Whatever comes up take it well, take it gaily. It's all in the luck
of the game.
Look for the best and the good things in life and you'll find in a
strange sort of way,
They come to the one who can greet every morning expecting a
wonderful day.

Twenty-first

It's hard to think of something fresh to say
When somebody is twenty-one today.
It's all been said before so many times
With all the old familiar worn-out rhymes.

And so it's just the same old thing once more.
I wish you health and lots of luck in store.
May Time be kind and Life be good to you.
I hope you'll reach your goal – and dreams come true.
But most of all I hope that you will find
The secret of a wise and happy mind.
For what's the use of money or success
Without the precious pearl of happiness?

Far Away

Far away – by distance reckoned – yet how near you seem to
me!
Separated, yet together in the realms of Memory.

Far away, but here in thought. The miles between us melt
away . . .
Parted, yet in spirit meeting – every hour of every day.

Best Points

Look out for the best points in others,
Look out for the finest things first . . .
Be sure that you've found all the good traits
Before recognising the worst.

Too often, put out by some quarrel
Past kindness we're apt to forget
The ties of affection are severed
By words that we live to regret.

And many a friendship is broken,
Because when it comes to the test
We see only what are the worst points
And fail to remember the best.

Moss

Along the garden path between the worn and crumbling stone,
There are strips of velvet where the soft green moss has grown.

And here and there upon Life's path a broken stone appears.
Yet time is kind – and in the crazy paving of the years,
It covers up the ugly cracks and hides them from our sight,
With the moss of sweet remembrance, ever green and bright.

The Faithful Heart

Faithful to the promise given, now and through the days to be.
Bound by ties of fond affection – and the cords of memory.
Absence proves the heart's devotion – testing Love's
                                        sincerity . . .
Steadfast in a world of chaos – shines the star of constancy.

Never

Never give up hoping. There's nothing to be lost.
Never give up trying, however great the cost.
Never give up climbing, though clouds obscure the view.
Never give up striving, your purpose to pursue.

Never give up trusting the hand of Providence
To lead and guide you safely through every circumstance.
Never give up praying whatever else you do.
Never give up saying that all is well with you.
This is faith dynamic, the power most wonderful,
The faith that moves the mountain and works the miracle.

Hope Deferred

Do not be despondent when your hopes have been deferred,
And it seems your prayers have gone unheeded or unheard.
Do not be discouraged when your wish has not come true.
Never lose your faith. Be patient. Take the longer view.

Give God time. It's not for you to say just when and where
You want a thing to happen, for the answer to a prayer
Must sometimes be delayed because the Providential schemes
Are wider than the expectations of your dearest dreams.
So learn to wait and learn to trust and never cease to pray.
Often do we find there was a blessing in delay.

Traffic

Traffic is people. Traffic's more than fumes and wheels and
                                                    noise.
Traffic is women, men and children. Traffic is girls and boys.
People who are dear to someone. Life is sweet to all.
So take no risk and never let your highest standards fall.

Be courteous to others and consideration show
To those with whom you share the road; with care and caution
                                                    go,
Remembering your obligations when you ride or drive.
Traffic is people, like yourself, who want to stay alive.

Let There Be Light

Where there is ignorance – let there be knowledge.
Where hearts are blind and hard, let there be sight.
Where there is falsity – let truth be uttered.
Where evil casts its gloom let there be light.

Exercising the Will

Exercise your will each day to keep it firm and strong
So that you can make decisions, sifting right from wrong . . .
If you do not work your will-power it will atrophy.
Like a limb that's never used, quite useless it will be.

Be Assured

When you give in to despair, you doubt God in your soul.
But remember He is God, and He is in control.
Do you think He has forgotten all your secret prayers?
Be assured He knows it all. He loves you and He cares.

To Your Highest Self Be True

Did you fail to reap good crops when came life's harvest-tide?
Have you failed to reach the mark? And have you been denied
The fulfilment of your dreams? It may seem so to you –
But you have not failed if to yourself you have been true.

Thirsting By the Well

Life's a hard and dusty road, but here and there along the way
There are wells of living water, so that in the heat of day
Man can quench his thirst for God . . . and yet how often we
                                                        pass by
Heedless of the green oases underneath the brazen sky.

The Swing

Swing high,
Swing low,
Up to the top of the tree you go,
Seeing the mill at the water's edge,
Seeing for miles over field and hedge.

Swing high,
Swing low,
Down to the ground and then up you go.
Catching a glimpse of the old green pond,
The church in the lane and the woods beyond.

Swing high,
Swing low,
Just like a bird on the wing you go.
But what would you say if the swing swung high,
And left you up there in the bright blue sky?

Pamela Jane

Pamela Jane was caught in the rain,
When walking one Sunday in Sparepenny Lane.
She didn't know whether to hurry and run
Or stand under shelter and wait for the sun.

She found a dry spot where the trees made a roof,
But soon even that was not quite waterproof.
The leaves dropped big splashes that fell pit-a-pat
Right on the top of her very best hat.

Crash went the thunder and down came the hail.
But I've forgotten the end of the tale.
So we must leave her out there in the rain.
Oh what a pity! Poor Pamela Jane.

Mother and Son

I used to take you in my arms and kiss your tears away.
When you were hurt you ran to me. But that was yesterday –
Then you were a little boy and all my very own.
Now you are a man and you must learn to stand alone.

Sometimes when I see that there are troubles on your mind,
I long to bear your burdens and I wish that I could find
A way to show my love for you. But what help can I be?
The years have passed and you have grown beyond your need
of me.

Lazy Days

If you're on your feet all day with little time to sit,
Have a lazy holiday and make a rest of it . . .
Don't go rushing here and there, but take things easily,
In some quiet country place or down beside the sea.

Many tonics can be bought, but fresh air is the best.
Take a course of Nature's treatment, have a lovely rest.
Then when you are back again inside life's busy maze,
You will feel the benefit of all those lazy days.

Perhaps

If a record could be made
Of every wedding, to be played
In times of crisis and of stress
To recall past happiness,
Perhaps more marriages would be
Rescued from calamity.

Once again unhappy pairs
Could hear the pledges and the prayers;
The sacred vows they made that day –
To love, to honour and obey.

The Lodestar

You are the lodestar of my life. Your love is like the guiding
light
That brings the mariner to harbour through the darkness of the
night.
The great ships set their course for home, and on that constant
star rely
Led by the eternal lamp that burns upon the northern sky.

You are the dream I have pursued across the oceans of the
years.
You are my hope and my salvation. Yours is the love that
calms all fears.
You are my star of fate and fortune, steadfast, unfailing,
changeless, true.
Safely I'm brought to quiet havens when in my heart I turn to
you.

Something to Give

We all have something to give the world – and nobody else but
                                                              you
Can perform the task that it was destined you should do.
So never feel that you are just a unit in a crowd.
You are an individual with special gifts endowed.

It may be just the gift of spreading cheerful thoughts about –
Or keeping calm when there's a fuss and smoothing troubles
                                                         out . . .
We all have parts to play no matter where or how we live.
We all have something to offer life. We all have something to
                                                            give.

Moods

April keeps us guessing with her sunshine and her showers.
In the wake of storms she brings the rainbow and the flowers.
First she smiles a radiant smile and then she frowns and broods.
It is hard to keep up with her ever-changing moods.

Do not be like April, one day bright, the next in tears,
Always at the mercy of your moods, your hopes and fears . . .
Live life in the sunshine of a gay philosophy
One that does not vary with the winds of destiny.

Pleasures Unsought

The loveliest song I ever heard
Came from the throat of a tiny bird,
When a torrent of lark notes pure and high
Poured through the quiet of the downland sky.

The loveliest picture I ever saw
Was something no artist could paint or draw –
When the moon trailed a streamer of silver light
Over the sea on a summer's night.

The loveliest things it seems to me,
When looking back in memory,
Are those that we do not seek or find
By an effort of the mind:
The beauty glimpsed, the music caught.
The pleasures that come to us unsought.

Let It Pass and Let It Go

Do not hang on to a grievance. Let it pass and let it go.
Do not cling to hurts and grudges. Life is very short, you
know.
Bear no malice, never harbour thoughts of bitterness or spite –
Whether you are in the wrong or whether you are in the right.
You can't afford to let the poison seep right down into your
mind.
Try to think of something else and very quickly you will find
The trouble loses its importance and in time will fade away.
So if something riles and rankles turn it out without delay.

You must take the generous view however much you've been
upset.
You've got to let the grievance go. You've got to drop it and
forget.
If you're hard and unforgiving in the things you do and say
How much mercy can *you* hope for on the final judgment day?

The Blessings of the Years

Do not count the passing years, but count your friends instead,
Remembering the old friends and the new.
Do not count the milestones as the road of life you tread –
But the good things God has given you.

Don't add up the birthdays as they come and as they go –
With vain regrets that Time flies all too fast . . .
Count the happy memories that set your heart aglow;
The blessings of the present and the past.

Here at the Gate

I want a new dream, a new hope, a new heart.
I'd like to be able to make a fresh start –
With nothing to worry or weigh on my mind –
Mistakes all forgiven, the past left behind.

Here at the gate where a new year begins,
I wish I could shed all my sorrows and sins,
But Life's not like that. Though you tread a new track,
The old load you still have to bear on your back.

You can't drop that burden. It's still yours to bear,
But this you can do; you can start with a prayer –
Not to be given an easier load
But a new vision to light the old road.

Resolution

I will do what life demands, whatever it may be –
I will work with willing hands, and conscientiously
Strive to put the best I know into the task I do.
With God's help I will be faithful, steadfast, just and true.

Communion

Busy I shall be this day, but I must vow to take
A quiet moment here and there, a secret prayer to make.
Moments of communion we need from hour to hour
To draw from God the things we need: hope, courage, grace
and power.

Eyes to See

Behind the turmoil of the world with all its clamourings,
May we always strive to hear the rush of angel wings . . .
Behind the common scenes of life, though drab they seem to be,
Shines the glory of the Lord for all with eyes to see.

Stronger Shoes

Do not ask for smoother pathways, but for stronger shoes to
                                                        wear,
So that you can climb the mountains, and a heavy burden
                                                    bear . . .
Do not wish for easy times, but for a greater courage pray –
So that you can meet with joy whatever comes with every day.

The Silent Garden

Silent now the garden lies
Under dark and stormy skies.
Days are short and nights are long,
Frosts are sharp and winds are strong . . .
One by one the petals fall
From the last rose on the wall.
Winter's breath is in the air;
Birds are mute and boughs are bare.

Yet no bitter tear we shed,
For we know they are not dead.
We, with faith unquestioning,
Say there'll be another Spring.
At the end of Winter's reign,
In the garden once again,
There'll be blossom on the spray.
None can take this hope away.

Why then should our faith sink low,
When some loved one has to go
Out into the great unknown –
Out into the dark alone?
Death the victor may appear.
But remember, year by year,
New sap rises in the tree.
Life goes on eternally.

My Quest

Thy truth I seek – no other quest is worth the toil and agony.
Thy love I seek – no other love can satisfy me utterly.
Thy joy I seek – Thy joy is life, is hope and health and energy.
Thyself I seek – for Thou art God and every good exists in
Thee.

Resurrection

Round the dark and troubled world the bells of Easter ring,
Bringing to our weary hearts the message of the Spring.
Season of awakening, renewal and rebirth,
Mystic resurrection of the glory of the earth.

Hope revives and joy returns and faith is now reborn
In the light that cometh with the resurrection morn . . .
As we hail the risen Christ His image we can see,
Shining through the loveliness of field and flower and tree.

Pledge of immortality in every living thing,
Promise of eternal life in seed and leaf and wing . . .
Love has triumphed over Death. The stone is rolled away.
God has granted unto us another Easter Day.

Nature's Wonderland

For all our vaunted cleverness we cannot understand
The beauty and the mystery of Nature's wonderland.
The sun, the moon, the whirling stars, the sea, the sky, the
earth –
All the many miracles of life and death and birth.

Man with marvellous machines can do stupendous things
But could not with his hands create a bird with voice and
wings.
Could not make a rose, a rainbow, or a common weed,
A chrysalis, a dragonfly, a cabbage or a seed.

Cannot say what magic holds the planet in its place
Or how the spider spins its dainty web of fairy lace . . .
He cannot make a blade of grass, a leaf, a cone, a pod
Yet he is too arrogant to give the praise to God.

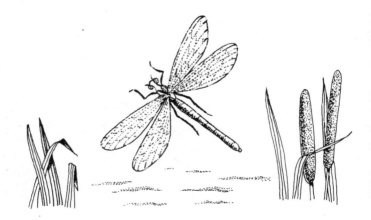

Tomorrow

Do not let your faith be shaken by the touch of sorrow,
But remember God is good and there will be tomorrow . . .
All must strive and suffer – that's the way it has to be.
Life's a skein of twisted threads: joy, laughter, tragedy.

Never doubt. Hold on and hope though hope seems all in vain.
Sooner than you think perhaps the sun will shine again . . .
Troubles and misfortunes come to put you to the test,
Proving strength or weakness, bringing out the worst and best.

No one wants to weep with you if you are always sad.
Lonely you will never be if you are brave and glad . . .
Search the clouds – you're bound to find a gleam of light to
                                        follow
Though today is grim and grey . . . remember there's
                                        tomorrow.

Baby's Hand

There are many lovely things: stars, rainbows, birds and trees,
Roses, mountains, butterflies, the skies, the earth, the seas,
Petals, dewdrops, cones and berries, seeds and shells and sand –
But nothing half so lovely as a baby's little hand.

Just a scrap of dimpled flesh, a tiny, tender thing,
Softer than the silken feathers on a linnet's wing,
Thumb and fingers, veins and nails, a perfect work of art.
Weak, and yet it has the power to move the hardest heart.

Many busy hands we'll need our better world to build –
If the hopes for which we've suffered are to be fulfilled.
So when you see a baby's hand take hold of it and pray –
That God will use it for His work somehow, somewhere,
                                                    someday.

Wedding Rings

Engagement rings may vary as to price and size and kind –
Diamonds, sapphires, pearls and rubies, many types you find,
But wedding rings all look alike in platinum or gold.
No matter what they cost to buy, or whether new or old,
They all look very much the same upon a woman's hand –
Plain and unpretentious, just a little simple band.
Yet every one is different, for every one you see
Has a story of its own, a secret history.
The tiny hoop, although so small, holds all the world for two,
Enclosing them within the circle of a dream come true.

He Planted a Tree

He planted a tree in memory of his beloved wife.
When she went, it seemed that there was nothing left in life.
Nothing but the dear remembrance of the days gone by:
The happy days before Death came to break Love's golden tie.

But year by year, the tree he planted grows before his eyes,
And every springtime, when the new leaves open to the skies,
It seems to bring a promise of the life that is to be.
And his heart draws comfort from the Tree of Memory.

The Acrobat

I love to watch the bluetit with his promise-tinted front –
Turning crazy somersaults. It's like a circus stunt . . .
Upside down he hangs and pecks a juicy bit of fat.
No mistake about it, he's a first–class acrobat.

Watch him with the monkey nuts. He has the greatest fun.
He swings and clings and picks the precious nuts out one by
one.
Agile as a star performer on a high trapeze,
He jerks and jiggles, twists and wriggles with the utmost ease.
And when a bit of coconut is hung out on the tree,
With his claws he gets a grip and nibbles skilfully.
It's as if he sets out to amuse and entertain.
I do believe he knows we're watching at the windowpane.

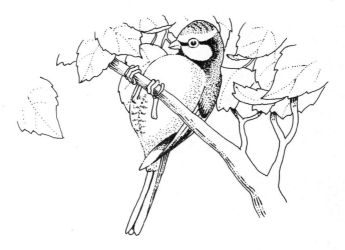

Prayer

Prayer changes funk into courage. Prayer changes night into
day.
Prayer changes gloom into glory and pushes the mountains
away.
Prayer changes everything somehow in ways that we can't
understand.
Prayer makes us wiser and stronger to cope with life's daily
demand.

Prayer is the link that connects us with God in His heaven
above.
Prayer brings us into the presence of Him who is power, life
and love.

Regrets

There's always something to regret, however much you've
done

To help to make life happier for a beloved one.
However deep your grief may be, thoughts come to trouble you
When there's no more you can say and nothing you can do.

You recall misunderstandings; trivialities
Steal out of the past to spoil the sweetest memories,
Things that haunt the house of sorrow, things you can't forget.
So lose no chance to prove your love. Have nothing to regret.

Doubts

Doubts breed in the shadows when the lamp of Faith burns
                                                    low.
Doubts creep up out of the darkness and in strength they grow,
Crawling from the secret places, thriving in the gloom.
One by one they take possession of the inner room.

Once the glow of Faith is dimmed, the doubts will multiply
Until there is no corner left for Hope to occupy.
So keep alight the lamp of Faith, for in its steady beam
Doubts will vanish like the phantoms of an evil dream.

Have a Heart

Have a heart that tries to feel what other people feel.
Have a heart – a sympathetic word will often heal
The hurt of one who stoops beneath a weight that none will
                                                    share,
With nobody to lend a hand and nobody to care.

The world is full of people needing all that you can give.
Old folks feeling lonely with a few brief years to live.
Children badly treated, all around you everywhere
Are sufferers with trials to face and crosses they must bear.
They need your love. They need your strength, they need your
                                                    kindly hands.
So have a heart, a heart that feels – a heart that understands.

Learning to Live

It's a hard and a difficult business, this business of learning to
live,
Knowing how best to make use of the knowledge that the
passing years give.
To muster the technique of living is something not learnt in a
day,
For only experience teaches and time alone shows us the way.

It's an art to be studied and practised, to achieve a degree of
success.
It's a ding–dong of trial and error: some succeed – others never
progress.
It takes time to discover the right way of coping with people
and things,
And it's not until life is half over that we learn how to take
what it brings.

Magic

There's a magic about the sea: it casts its own strange spells
On the lonely shores among the rocks and pools and shells.
By harbours where the fishermen spread out their nets to dry,
And at the gay resorts with all the traffic roaring by.

There's a fascination watching waves by day and night
Curling softly on the sand or breaking foamy white.
On windy cliff or crowded beach, by quiet cave or quay,
It's there; the ancient magic of the everlasting sea.

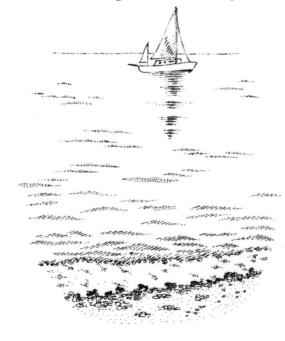

My Friends

Fate has often led my footsteps to a place of destiny,
Where I found a kindred spirit, someone waiting there for me.

For all other precious things I've searched and struggled,
worked and fought,
But my friends, the best and dearest, these have come to me
unsought.

A Sense of Humour

If you see the funny side, you'll stroll along the sunny side
While other folk are walking in the shade.
Things will never harass you, embitter or embarrass you.
A sense of humour is the finest aid
To wisdom and philosophy. In trouble and adversity
It brings you smiling through the stress and strife.
So cultivate the power to see – the little touch of comedy
Behind the trials and tragedies of life.

A Seat in the Sun

It's known in the town as the Grandfathers' Seat,
And on days that are sunny and fair
The same little group of old folks can be seen,
Sitting enjoying the air.
Smoking and joking and nodding a bit,
Watching the crowds hurry on.
Sifting old memories, thinking long thoughts.
Talking of times that are gone.
God grant all grandfathers joy and content
And peace when their life's work is done.
For what could be better than this at the end?
A pipe . . . and a seat in the sun.

It Helps

It helps to talk things over if you're anxious or afraid
When hurt or worried, and there are decisions to be made,
Problems though gigantic tend to dwindle when discussed.
It helps to open up your heart to someone you can trust.

Someone sympathetic who will listen and advise.
Someone who will share your trouble – someone kind and wise.
When there's a tangle to untie and life makes hard demands
It helps to talk it over with a friend who understands.

Roses Everywhere

Here again comes lovely June! No place on earth can show
Such beauty as our Britain in the summer's early glow.
Washed by softly falling rains the grass grows greener here
And where else on this globe does Heaven seem to be so near?

Carpeted with buttercups the golden meadows blaze.
Wild flowers flow along the verges of the country ways.
Bright is every cottage garden in the winding lanes
With jasmine and with honeysuckle at the windowpanes.
Gardens bright with candy-tuft, with thrift and irises.
Pathways edged with lupins, pansies, pinks and peonies.
Stocks in rainbow tinges that cast their sweetness on the air.
And roses white, pink, gold and crimson. Roses everywhere.

The Best

The best is never over, there is always something new,
Another start, another chance, another road for you.
Another mountain top to climb though hopeless it may seem.
A fresh adventure beckoning, another dream to dream.

The best is never buried with the ashes of the past.
The best is where you look for it. No happiness can last
But other joys are granted if you press on faithfully,
Believing in the promises that 'the best is yet to be'.

Time Is Life

You can't buy or borrow a minute. Time isn't for sale. Time is
Life.
Yet how we squander and waste it – in worry and folly and
strife
And things of no value or merit – the pleasures that die with the
day.
If Time were for sale how we'd treasure the hours that we
fritter away!

Spend Time as you spend gold or silver. Spend wisely what
Time God may give.
Time wasted is Time gone forever. It can't be recalled to relive.
And when at the last Time grows precious and Time is the
thing that you lack
You think of lost friends and lost chances and the days that will
never come back.

Life Is Now

You can't put life aside, for life is now. Life is today.
Life is not tomorrow and you cannot turn away
From problems and experiences that you have never sought,
Just because you're unprepared for what the day has brought.

You've got to deal with every moment as it comes along
Making your decisions wise or foolish, right or wrong.
Life won't wait until you've got things sorted out somehow.
You've got to live it, ready or unready. Life is now.

On the Way

Here come snowdrops once again; they look so small and frail,
Yet how sturdily they stand against the wintry gale.
Set on stalks of tender green, they swing their fairy bells,
Grouped about the gates of Lent, like ghostly sentinels.

Once the snowdrops have arrived, a change they seem to bring.
The days begin to lengthen and the birds begin to sing.
The earth may still be frosted and the skies be wild and grey,
But the snowdrops whisper that the Spring is on the way.

The Happy Life

All men seek the happy life; down many roads they fare,
Searching for a pleasant path away from strife and care,
Looking for some hidden turning where the sunlight gleams,
Following their star of fortune down the track of dreams.

Restless, never satisfied, life's winding ways they wend,
Always thinking there'll be something better round the bend –
Pressing on towards some distant castle in the blue,
Never pausing where they stand, the present scene to view.

Learn to live each passing day as if it were the last:
Do not dwell in thought upon the future or the past.
It is good to dream a dream; it helps you on your way –
But remember you can live the happy life . . . Today.

A Foothold

Home is a foothold in the world, a spot that we can make our
own.
Who'd want to be a wanderer, a restless soul, a rolling stone?
The world is big; too big for me. I have no wish to rove or
roam.
Give me four walls, I care not where, and I will make myself a
home.

Sunward

Keep on looking sunward although the skies are grey.
Keep on looking forward towards a brighter day . . .
Clouds may frown above you, but always keep an eye
On the golden edges that gild the stormy sky.

Keep your thoughts turned sunward and dwell on happy things.
Let your hopes rise upward like birds on soaring wings.
Face the right direction until the sun appears.
Turn towards the brightness, away from doubts and fears.

Green Fingers

Some have green fingers . . . their gardens will thrive.
In every weather their plants will survive.
Soil may be poor and the air may be cold,
Yet 'neath green fingers – bulbs shoot and unfold,
Defying the foes that attack other flowers,
Seeming to grow by miraculous powers . . .
Blight cannot touch them and pests cannot harm,
Held in the spell of some magical charm.

What is the reason? Does anyone know
Why one will die and the other will grow?
Flowers have their feelings. Yes, Flowers understand –
If there is love in the touch of a hand.

Dark Cupboards

I have planted my bulbs in their bright coloured bowls,
And I've put them away in the gloom
Of a little dark cupboard; it's hard to believe
That they'll live in the darkness, and bloom
In a glory of purple, of white and of pink,
From those small thread-like roots in the mould.
I shall watch the great miracle under my eyes
As the close-clustered petals unfold.
There are dark little cupboards in everyone's life
Where we hide all our secrets away –
Griefs, grudges and fears and frustrated desires
Thrust aside from the light of the day.
Could we open our cupboards and bring them all out
Of the darkness – perhaps we should find
The green tips of friendship – fresh flowers of new hope
Growing out of the depths of the mind.

The Tempter

When hope sinks low and courage fails and everything seems
                                                    wrong,
That's the fatal moment when the devil comes along,
Tempting you to doubt God's goodness and your faith deny –
That's when you must be on guard, the tempter to defy.

He's always there, the trouble-maker, looking for a chance
To weaken you, to trip you up and hinder your advance.
He's always near you, whispering and plucking at your sleeve.
So when tempted to give in, stand fast, hold on – believe.

Courtesy

It smooths the path and oils the wheels, a little courtesy.
It sweetens our relationships. How different life would be,
If everyone would be polite, considerate and kind.
It would help to ease the hardships of the daily grind.

It doesn't cost us anything, and yet it means so much;
The tone of affability, the sympathetic touch;
The civil word, the charming manner; geniality –
Showing unto friend and stranger simple courtesy.

Fairy Castles

Planning for the future, and dreaming golden dreams!
That's what keeps us going; a foolish thing it seems,
But all men have their longings and treasure silently
Their own idea of Heaven, and happy days to be.

It is these secret visions that keep our hopes awake.
Without something to live for the heart would surely break.
It speeds the laggard moments and helps us struggle through –
To plan our fairy castles and build them in the blue.

Sewing

In and out the needle goes along the folded seam,
While your heart is following some lost and lovely dream.
In between the stitches you can go a long, long way,
When you're sitting sewing at the quiet end of day.

O, the things that you remember as you draw the thread!
Odds and ends of memory come back into your head.
Names and faces, times and places, round the world you go.
Many miles you travel as you watch the stitches grow.

The Great Thought

Lean upon the thought of God, a great thought let it be,
Large enough and deep enough to rest in, utterly.
Finding consolation, hope, refreshment and release
In the quiet comfort of His presence and His peace.

Lean on this, for this alone will take your whole full weight.
And will make you strong to face whatever be your fate.
Every other staff and stay will be of no avail.
Lean upon the word of God for this will never fail.

The Lamp

The Word of God is like a lamp. It shines upon the unknown
way –
And sends into the darkest place, a steady glow, a guiding ray.
Light Eternal burning ever as towards the Truth men grope –
Leading them by hidden ways along the paths of faith and
hope.

While You're Waiting

While you're waiting for tomorrow, get the best out of today.
While you're waiting for the sunshine don't complain at skies of
grey.
While you wait for future pleasures don't forget the ones you've
had.
Call to mind the things enjoyed, the happy times and not the
sad.

While you're waiting for the granting of the wish you hold most
dear,
Don't lose sight of all the joys that life can offer now and here.
Times of waiting can be fruitful and to you much good can
bring.
Make the winter yield a blessing while you're waiting for the
Spring.

Dividends

Make Life pay dividends. You can if you choose,
For it's a business. You gain or you lose.
Though you have problems and troubles to meet –
Don't accept failure and loss and defeat.

Profit by everything. Wrest good from ill.
Double your assets of wisdom and skill.
Turn to advantage whatever Fate sends.
Increase your happiness. Add to your friends.

Showing the World

If you've a song,
Try it.
If you've a tear,
Dry it.
If you've a cross,
Bear it.
If you've a joy,
Share it.
When Hope grows faint,
Brace it.
When trouble comes,
Face it.

Where there's a wrong,
Right it.
When life is grim,
Fight it.
If you've a hand,
Give it,
If you've a creed,
Live it.
If you've a faith,
Show it.
And let the world
Know it.

Dreamer

Dreaming of the things you mean to do some other day.
Always dreaming of tomorrow, wishing Time away.
Dreaming of the happiness that is eluding you.
Never doing anything to make the dream come true.

Dreaming of the lovely things you think you want or need.
Dreaming of the roses, never working at the weed.
Dreaming of a goal but never shouldering a load –
And really setting out to face the hazards of the road.

Dreaming of a harvest when you never touch a plough.
Dreaming of the future and forgetting Life is NOW.

Colouring

Colours make the beauty of the earth and of the sky.
Grass-green meadows, clay-brown land and white clouds
floating by.
Golden dawns and rosy sunsets and the lovely tones –
Of colourings in gems and jewels, shells and rocks and stones.

Garden flowers and country flowers in varied rainbow hues:
Pinks and purples, grey and silver, lavenders and blues . . .
What are colours? How would you define them to the blind,
So that they imagining, could see them in the mind?
Yellow corn and wine-dark rose, a butterfly's bright wing.
How could you explain in words this thing called colouring?

Seeing

The eyes are wonderful indeed, for with them you can see
Big things like a sun, a moon, a mountain or a tree –
And little things like glow-worms, seeds and dewdrops
                                    diamond-bright.
Marvellous beyond all telling is the gift of sight.

You see a vision of the world as through a pane of glass –
And those outside can see your thoughts as through the mind
                                    they pass;
Anger, sorrow, joy: the greatest brain could not devise –
So clever a contrivance as the windows of the eyes.

Looking at Life

Don't condemn the world because you don't like what you see:
Trouble and unhappiness, greed, vice and misery . . .
Certainly these things exist and cannot be denied –
But don't forget that there is something on the other side:
Courage and unselfishness and much that's good and kind.
It really all depends upon the focus of your mind.

Don't let dark distorting shadows spoil the world for you.
The fault may lie within yourself, so change your point of
view.
Instead of looking on the bad and dwelling on the worst –
Try to get a broader vision, putting best things first . . .
Turn the camera round: a different angle strike.
You will get another picture – maybe one you'll like.

Aspect

If you build a house, consider aspect first of all.
Do not let the sunbeams play upon a solid wall . . .
Plan your windows so that every room with light is blessed –
Catching all the brightness as the sun moves east to west.

Thoughts like windows must be made to face the brightest
way.
Set them in the right direction when you plan your day.
Providence may smile on you or fortune seem unkind.
So much will depend upon the aspect of your mind.

Turn yourself away from things that anger and depress.
Do not live behind a wall of grief or bitterness.
Break it with a window that will open up a view.
Face the way the sun is shining. Let the light get through.

Let There Be Peace

Keep the peace within your soul, unmoved and unafraid.
Face the worst that life can do, by nothing be dismayed.
Build an inner sanctuary of secret happiness –
Rise above your daily worries, fretful thoughts suppress.

Try to make an inner world of faith and quietude –
A temple of tranquillity where strength can be renewed –
Where joy can grow and hope unfold and confidence increase.
Outside may be conflict . . . but within let there be peace.

When Sorrows Come

We wonder why it has to be when sorrow comes our way –
The horizons of the morrow turn from gold to grey . . .
All the lovely things we dreamed of vanish overnight –
Looking out along the road we see no gleam of light.

Where then can we look for hope to break the dark despair –
When the cross of our affliction seems too hard to bear?
Where then can we turn for consolation and relief?
Where find blame to ease the heart and heal the wound of grief?

Only in the knowledge that all things are transient.
Nothing in this changing world is fixed or permanent.
It is but the shadow of the great reality –
A place of preparation for the life that is to be.

To a Colleague on Retirement

We're sorry you are leaving us. We'll miss you every day
But all must reach this turning point upon life's winding way.
The time has come to leave the desk at which you've worked
and won
The warm affection and the real respect of everyone.

So congratulations! May the future bring to you
Many blessings, many friends, and life begin anew . . .
We wish you health and happiness and all prosperity.
Your task here may be finished, but 'the best is yet to be'.

The Joy of Gardens

In a fair and fragrant garden God created Man.
It must have been His wish for us, His purpose and His plan –
That we should learn to love the trees, the birds, the grass, the
                                                              flowers.
The story of the race begins in Eden's pleasant bowers.

The love of gardens still remains a joy that never dies
For the poor man and the rich; the simple and the wise . . .
Whether it be planted in a wide or narrow space
He who makes a garden makes the world a sweeter place.

The Mystery of Prayer

We know not what we do when for our absent ones we pray.
We know not how the magic works – but somewhere far away
Someone receives a blessing, and is comforted
Silently around their path the angel wings are spread.

Though from them we are divided. Love will bridge the gap.
We know not what strange powers we touch, what secret
springs we tap
When we kneel and earnestly commit them to God's care.
Great things are accomplished through the mystery of prayer.

Green Is My Garden

Green is my garden and gay are the flowers.
Lovely the trees in the sun and the showers.
But what can I do with these midsummer hours,
Without you?

Red are the roses that bloom on the wall.
Sweet is the music when morning birds call.
But there is a sigh at the heart of it all –
Without you.

A Glimpse of England

Water-meadows rich and green where herds of cattle graze.
An old stone bridge round which there clings a dream of
                                        bygone days . . .
Streams where pollard willows stoop and graceful swans glide
                                                        by.
Pools that hold the lights and shadows of the changing sky.

Across the fields the Minster towers rise up as if to crown
The quaint old streets and houses of the little market town.
This is what we fought for! For this we shall hold fast.
The beauty that is England – and the glory of the Past.

Look Forward

Look forward and your hopes will rise.
Look forward!
Though stormy clouds frown in the skies.
Look forward!
The steps of Time you can't retrace
Press onward at an eager pace
Towards some finer, fairer place –
Look forward!

Look forward with a hopeful mind.
Look forward!
Resolve to leave the past behind.
Look forward!
You can't afford to let your gaze
Turn back to rest on other days.
Down brighter, better, broader ways
Look forward!

Safe Keeping

I pray for your safe keeping with every hour that chimes
Through all the pain and peril and terror of the times . . .
My thoughts are ever with you although we are apart –
In daytime and in darkness, you're in my mind and heart.

We cannot be together these troubled hours to share.
But may you be protected. This is my constant prayer.
Though dark the days of danger and dire the storm and strain.
God have you in His keeping until we meet again.

Wild Forget-me-nots

When bees hum in the linden tree and roses bloom in cottage
plots
Along the brookside banks we see the blue of wild forget-me-
nots.

Shy flowers that shun the prying eye – content to let the daisy
hold,
The glances of the passers-by – with brazen stare of white and
gold.

Forget-me-not! From long ago it stirs the thought of happier
days
For memories like wild flowers grow – along the heart's
untrodden ways.

Judgments

Don't judge with haste your fellow men – see only what is true.
Ignore the worst, bring out the best, and take the charitable
view.

I hope God does the same for us, and sees the virtues, not the
vice.
If He remembered only faults – who'd ever get to Paradise?

Thoughts Go Home

Thoughts go home unbidden when we're somewhere far away.
Thoughts need no compelling, off they wander night or day
To see the places and the faces dear unto the heart –
The spot where all our journeys end, and all roads end and
                                                    start.

Thoughts go back, they know the way. They need no goad or
                                                    guide
To cross the hills and rivers or the oceans that divide.
And though with friends we may abide, wherever we may
                                                    roam
To the place of heart's desire thoughts turn . . . love leads them
                                                    home.

The Sun Is Old

The sun is old, as old as Time, but every dawn is new.
The light of all created life has burned in heaven's blue
Since that first sweet daybreak when the sun sent down its rays
On a green and sinless world of fresh untrodden ways.

The sun is old, beyond the span of mortal reckoning
Yet every golden sunrise is a new and glorious thing.
Every time the morning glory lights your windowpane –
It can be a new beginning. Life can start again.

The Shallows and the Deeps

Quiet and shallow are the waters where the leafy willows
sway.
Yet this little winding river flowing gently on its way
Is going out to meet the sea and swell the ocean's rolling tide.
The stream will widen to embrace the mighty waves where
great ships ride.

Uneventful life may seem, a narrow stream of nights and days
Yet somewhere in the future it will open into broader ways.
Every soul in God's own time is called unto its destiny –
To steer its course alone upon the waters of Eternity.